W9-BMW-897

GREAT ENGLISH POETS

GREAT ENGLISH POETS

Percy Bysshe Shelley

Selected and with an introduction
by Peter Porter

Clarkson Potter/ Publishers
New York

Published in the United States by Clarkson N. Potter, Inc.
201 East 50th Street, New York, New York 10022
Member of the Crown Publishing Group. Random House, Inc.
New York, Toronto, London, Sydney, Auckland

Published in Great Britain by Aurum Press Ltd.
25 Bedford Street, London WC1 3AT

Picture research by Juliet Brightmore

Manufactured in Hong Kong

Library of Congress Cataloging-in-Publication Data

Shelley, Percy Bysshe, 1792-1822.
[Poems. Selections]
Percy Bysshe Shelley/selected and with an introduction by Peter
Porter. -- 1st ed.
p. cm -- (Great English poets)
I. Porter, Peter. II. Title. III. Series.
PR5403.P67   1994
821' .7--dc20   93-5584
CIP

ISBN 0-517-59648-2

10 9 8 7 6 5 4 3 2 1
First American Edition

CONTENTS

Introduction	10
From PROMETHEUS UNBOUND	
Spirit's Song	13
Song	14
'Music, when soft voices die'	17
'One word is too often profaned'	17
From EPIPSYCHIDION	18
From THE REVOLT OF ISLAM	21
From THE CENCI	
Beatrice Welcomes Death	24
Sonnet	25
Ozymandias	27
From THE MASK OF ANARCHY	28
From PETER BELL THE THIRD	
Hell	30
Song to the Men of England	34
Lines to a Critic	37
Sonnet: England in 1819	39
From LINES WRITTEN AMONG THE	
EUGANEAN HILLS	40
Stanzas Written in Dejection, Near Naples	42
From JULIAN AND MADDALO	45
With a Guitar, to Jane	48
From THE BOAT ON THE SERCHIO	52
From ADONAIS	
An Elegy on the Death of John Keats	55
From THE TRIUMPH OF LIFE	58
Sources of the extracts	60
Notes	61

INTRODUCTION

It is a paradox that Shelley and Byron, the most popular of the English Romantic poets, hardly deserve the description at all. Each lived a tempestuous life, and was a spectacularly visible embodiment of Romanticism, but each wrote in an older and more industrious tradition. You must look to Wordsworth, Coleridge and Keats for the real achievements of Romantic poetry.

There is a good case to be made out for considering Shelley a sort of Renaissance illuminatus like Erasmus or Francis Bacon, reborn at the end of the Enlightenment as a committed revolutionary. The Shelley whom the young Robert Browning hailed so enthusiastically in the 1840s ('O did you once see Shelley plain') was already passing into legend – the fated talent too idealistic for this world, whose legacy of beauty and frustration inspired generations of poets to exult in the power of literary romanticism. Later Victorians, such as Matthew Arnold, saw Shelley nostalgically, and perhaps more puritanically ('a beautiful and ineffectual angel'). By the end of the nineteenth century his reputation was transmuted into pure legend and his work played little part in the birth of Modern Poetry. However, his example of a pure spirit dying cruelly young has never been forgotten.

In all the legend-making, Shelley's poetry tends to be overlooked. He has not ceased to be a popular poet, and most people can quote famous lines from his works. 'To a Skylark', 'Ode to the West Wind' and 'Ozymandias' are in all the anthologies, and Shelley has fully lived up to that negative qualification for poetic fame, the adopting of his phrases and lines as titles for novels and plays – *Blithe*

Spirit, *If Winter Comes* and *Nurslings of Immortality*. Yet the long and passionately argued poems he laboured over are hardly persevered with: this most serious and programmatic of the English Romantics is valued for a handful of lyrical passages. But to argue this is to miss Shelley's true strength – he is one of the most 'thoughtful' of English poets. His originality lies in his putting reason to work on passion.

Shelley's large-scale poems, *Queen Mab*, *The Revolt of Islam*, and the unfinished *Triumph of Life*, are only intermittently up to the mark, but he attained greater success with his medium-length works. Not only his best writing but also his most original vision will be found in 'Julian and Maddalo', *Epipsychidion* and 'Lines Written Among the Euganean Hills'. To these examinations of the twin concerns of natural beauty and human love should be added his polemical and satirical poems, notably *The Mask of Anarchy* and *Peter Bell the Third*. Shelley's politics were practical, and he is a surprisingly effective propagandist. But he also had a companionable side, a charming man-of-the-world knowingness which pervades his poems of friendship. An attractive picture of Shelley and Byron together lies at the heart of 'Julian and Maddalo', which is subtitled 'A Conversation'.

Byron and Shelley found their true calling in Italy, and it would be hard to underestimate the influence of their sense of exile on their work. Much of Shelley's most beautiful writing is a testament to the 'Paradise of Exiles' which he observed with so exact and sympathetic an eye in Tuscany, the Campania and the Veneto. His intensely English poetry actually speaks with an Italian accent. Perhaps Shelley's deepest concern was with human love, as the passage from *Epipsychidion* on pages 18–20 shows.

Percy Bysshe Shelley was born in 1792, the grandson of a Sussex baronet. He hated Eton but was extremely well schooled in the classics, as well as speaking French, Italian and Spanish. He was sent down from Oxford for composing a pamphlet, *The Necessity of Atheism*, and became a follower of the philosopher William Godwin at a time when Anti-Jacobinism made any deviation from the orthodoxies of Church and State dangerous. After the collapse of his first marriage, he eloped with the teenage Mary Wollstonecraft Godwin (the philosopher's daughter).

Like Byron, he wrote most of his poetry in exile, firstly in Switzerland, where Mrs Shelley began *Frankenstein*, and then in Italy. He eagerly followed the political fortunes of the radicals in England, and wrote *The Mask of Anarchy* after learning of the massacre of working people at Peterloo in 1819. He and Mary lost several of their babies in the insanitary heat of Italy, and Shelley retreated more and more into poetic composition and into his dangerous preoccupation with sailing (he could not swim). His body was washed ashore in the Ligurian Gulf from his capsized boat in 1822, just before his thirtieth birthday, and was burned on the beach. His poetry was mostly published posthumously by Mary Shelley.

Because much of it is preserved in longer works, I have overall chosen extracts rather than complete poems. In some cases I have provided my own headings and sub-headings for extracted passages. Details of sources are given at the end of the book. To make the best use of the space available, I have given priority to somewhat neglected verses over perennial favourites such as 'To a Skylark', 'Ode to the West Wind' and 'The Sensitive Plant'.

From
PROMETHEUS UNBOUND

Spirit's Song

On a poet's lips I slept
Dreaming like a love-adept
In the sound his breathing kept;
Nor seeks nor finds he mortal blisses,
But feeds on the aëreal kisses
Of shapes that haunt thought's wildernesses.
He will watch from dawn to gloom
The lake-reflected sun illume
The yellow bees in the ivy-bloom,
Nor heed nor see, what things they be;
But from these create he can
Forms more real than living man,
Nurslings of immortality!

Song

Rarely, rarely, comest thou,
    Spirit of Delight!
Wherefore hast thou left me now
    Many a day and night?
Many a weary night and day
'Tis since thou art fled away.

How shall ever one like me
    Win thee back again?
With the joyous and the free
    Thou wilt scoff at pain.
Spirit false! thou hast forgot
    All but those who need thee not.

As a lizard with the shade
    Of a trembling leaf,
Thou with sorrow art dismayed;
    Even the sighs of grief
Reproach thee, that thou art not near,
And reproach thou wilt not hear.

Let me set my mournful ditty
    To a merry measure;
Thou wilt never come for pity,
    Thou wilt come for pleasure;
Pity then will cut away
Those cruel wings, and thou wilt stay.

I love all that thou lovest,
    Spirit of Delight!
The fresh Earth in new leaves dressed,
    And the starry night;
Autumn evening, and the morn
When the golden mists are born.

I love snow, and all the forms
    Of the radiant frost;
I love waves, and winds, and storms
    Everything almost
Which is Nature's, and may be
Untainted by man's misery.

I love tranquil solitude,
    And such society
As is quiet, wise, and good;
    Between thee and me
What difference? but thou dost possess
The things I seek, not love them less.

I love Love – though he has wings,
    And like light can flee,
But above all other things,
    Spirit, I love thee –
Thou art love and life! Oh, come,
Make once more my heart thy home.

Music, when soft voices die,
Vibrates in the memory –
Odours, when sweet violets sicken,
Live within the sense they quicken.

Rose leaves, when the rose is dead,
Are heaped for the belovèd's bed;
And so thy thoughts, when thou art gone,
Love itself shall slumber on.

🌿

One word is too often profaned
    For me to profane it,
One feeling too falsely disdained
    For thee to disdain it;
One hope is too like despair
    For prudence to smother,
And pity from thee more dear
    Than that from another.

I can give not what men call love,
    But wilt thou accept not
The worship the heart lifts above
    And the Heavens reject not –
The desire of the moth for the star,
    Of the night for the morrow,
The devotion to something afar
    From the sphere of our sorrow?

From EPIPSYCHIDION

Spouse! Sister! Angel! Pilot of the Fate
Whose course has been so starless! O too late
Belovèd! O too soon adored, by me!
For in the fields of Immortality
My spirit should at first have worshipped thine,
A divine presence in a place divine;
Or should have moved beside it on this earth,
A shadow of that substance, from its birth;
But not as now: – I love thee; yes, I feel
That on the fountain of my heart a seal
Is set, to keep its waters pure and bright
For thee, since in those *tears* thou hast delight.
We – are we not formed, as notes of music are,
For one another, though dissimilar;
Such difference without discord, as can make
Those sweetest sounds, in which all spirits shake
As trembling leaves in a continuous air?

Thy wisdom speaks in me, and bids me dare
Beacon the rocks on which high hearts are wrecked.
I never was attached to that great sect,
Whose doctrine is, that each one should select
Out of the crowd a mistress or a friend,
And all the rest, though fair and wise, commend

To cold oblivion, though it is in the code
Of modern morals, and the beaten road
Which those poor slaves with weary footsteps tread,
Who travel to their home among the dead
By the broad highway of the world, and so
With one chained friend, perhaps a jealous foe,
The dreariest and the longest journey go.

True Love in this differs from gold and clay,
That to divide is not to take away.
Love is like understanding, that grows bright,
Gazing on many truths; 'tis like thy light,
Imagination! which from earth and sky,
And from the depths of human fantasy,
As from a thousand prisms and mirrors, fills
The Universe with glorious beams, and kills
Error, the worm, with many a sun-like arrow
Of its reverberated lightning. Narrow
The heart that loves, the brain that contemplates,
The life that wears, the spirit that creates
One object, and one form, and builds thereby
A sepulchre for its eternity.

From THE REVOLT OF ISLAM

Man seeks for gold in mines, that he may
weave
A lasting chain for his own slavery; –
In fear and restless care that he may live
He toils for others, who must ever be
The joyless thralls of like captivity;
He murders, for his chiefs delight in ruin;
He builds the altar, that its idol's fee
May be his very blood; he is pursuing –
O, blind and willing wretch! – his own obscure
undoing.

Woman! – she is his slave, she has become
A thing I weep to speak – the child of scorn,
The outcast of a desolated home;
Falsehood, and fear, and toil, like waves have
worn
Channels upon her cheek, which smiles
adorn,
As calm decks the false Ocean: – well ye know,
What Woman is, for none of Woman born
Can choose but drain the bitter dregs of woe,
Which ever from the oppressed to the oppressors
flow.

This need not be; ye might arise, and will
That gold should lose its power, and thrones
their glory;
That love, which none may bind, be free to fill
The world, like light; and evil faith, grown
hoary
With crime, be quenched and die. – Yon
promontory
Even now eclipses the descending moon! –
Dungeons and palaces are transitory –
High temples fade like vapour – Man alone
Remains, whose will has power when all beside is
gone.

Beatrice Welcomes Death

Worse than despair,
Worse than the bitterness of death, is hope:
It is the only ill which can find place
Upon the giddy, sharp and narrow hour
Tottering beneath us. Plead with the swift frost
That it should spare the eldest flower of spring:
Plead with awakening earthquake, o'er whose
    couch
Even now a city stands, strong, fair, and free;
Now stench and blackness yawn, like death. Oh,
    plead
With famine, or wind-walking Pestilence,
Blind lightning, or the deaf sea, not with man!
Cruel, cold, formal man; righteous in words,
In deeds a Cain. No, Mother, we must die:
Since such is the reward of innocent lives;
Such the alleviation of worst wrongs.
And whilst our murderers live, and hard, cold men,
Smiling and slow, walk through a world of tears
To death as to life's sleep; 'twere just the grave
Were some strange joy for us. Come, obscure
    Death,
And wind me in thine all-embracing arms!
Like a fond mother hide me in thy bosom,
And rock me to the sleep from which none wake.

Sonnet

Lift not the painted veil which those who live
Call Life: though unreal shapes be pictured there,
And it but mimic all we would believe
With colours idly spread, – behind, lurk Fear
And Hope, twin Destinies; who ever weave
Their shadows, o'er the chasm, sightless and
    drear.
I knew one who had lifted it – he sought,
For his lost heart was tender, things to love,
But found them not, alas! nor was there aught
The world contains, the which he could approve.
Through the unheeding many he did move,
A splendour among shadows, a bright blot
Upon this gloomy scene, a Spirit that strove
For truth, and like the Preacher found it not.

Ozymandias

I met a traveller from an antique land
Who said: Two vast and trunkless legs of stone
Stand in the desert ... Near them, on the sand,
Half sunk, a shattered visage lies, whose frown,
And wrinkled lip, and sneer of cold command,
Tell that its sculptor well those passions read
Which yet survive, stamped on these lifeless
        things,
The hand that mocked them, and the heart that
        fed:
And on the pedestal these words appear:
'My name is Ozymandias, king of kings;
Look on my works, ye Mighty, and despair!'
Nothing beside remains. Round the decay
Of that colossal wreck, boundless and bare
The lone and level sands stretch far away.

From
THE MASK OF ANARCHY

As I lay asleep in Italy
There came a voice from over the Sea,
And with great power it forth led me
To walk in the visions of Poesy.

I met Murder on the way –
He had a mask like Castlereagh –
Very smooth he looked, yet grim;
Seven blood-hounds followed him:

All were fat; and well they might
Be in admirable plight,
For one by one, and two by two,
He tossed them human hearts to chew
Which from his wide cloak he drew.

Next came Fraud, and he had on,
Like Eldon, an ermined gown;
His big tears, for he wept well,
Turned to mill-stones as they fell.

And the little children, who
Round his feet played to and fro,
Thinking every tear a gem,
Had their brains knocked out by them.

Clothed with the Bible, as with light,
And the shadows of the night,
Like Sidmouth, next, Hypocrisy
On a crocodile rode by.

And many more Destructions played
In this ghastly masquerade,
All disguised, even to the eyes,
Like Bishops, lawyers, peers, or spies.

Last came Anarchy: he rode
On a white horse, splashed with blood;
He was pale even to the lips,
Like Death in the Apocalypse.

And he wore a kingly crown;
And in his grasp a sceptre shone;
On his brow this mark I saw –
'I AM GOD, AND KING, AND LAW!'

With a pace stately and fast,
Over English land he passed,
Trampling to a mire of blood
The adoring multitude.

And a mighty troop around,
With their trampling shook the ground,
Waving each a bloody sword,
For the service of their Lord.

And with glorious triumph, they
Rode through England proud and gay,
Drunk as with intoxication
Of the wine of desolation.

From PETER BELL THE THIRD

Hell

Hell is a city much like London –
  A populous and a smoky city;
There are all sorts of people undone,
And there is little or no fun done;
  Small justice shown, and still less pity.

There is a Castles, and a Canning,
  A Cobbett, and a Castlereagh;
All sorts of caitiff corpses planning
All sorts of cozening for trepanning
  Corpses less corrupt than they.

There is a Chancery Court; a King;
  A manufacturing mob; a set
Of thieves who by themselves are sent
Similar thieves to represent;
  An army; and a public debt.

Which last is a scheme of paper money,
  And means – being interpreted –
'Bees, keep your wax – give us the honey,
And we will plant, while skies are sunny,
  Flowers, which in winter serve instead.'

There is a great talk of revolution –
  And a great chance of despotism –

German soldiers – camps – confusion –
Tumults – lotteries – rage – delusion –
    Gin – suicide – and methodism;

Taxes too, on wine and bread,
    And meat, and beer, and tea, and cheese,
From which those patriots pure are fed,
Who gorge before they reel to bed
    The tenfold essence of all these.

There are mincing women, mewing,
    (Like cats, who *amant misere*,)
Of their own virtue, and pursuing
Their gentler sisters to that ruin,
    Without which – what were chastity?

Lawyers – judges – old hobnobbers
    Are there – bailiffs – chancellors –
Bishops – great and little robbers –
Rhymesters – pamphleteers – stock-jobbers –
    Men of glory in the wars, –

Things whose trade is, over ladies
    To lean, and flirt, and stare, and simper,
Till all that is divine in woman
Grows cruel, courteous, smooth, inhuman,
    Crucified 'twixt a smile and whimper.

Thrusting, toiling, wailing, moiling,
    Frowning, preaching – such a riot!

Each with never-ceasing labour,
Whilst he thinks he cheats his neighbour,
    Cheating his own heart of quiet.

And all these meet at levees; –
    Dinners convivial and political; –
Suppers of epic poets; – teas,
Where small talk dies in agonies; –
    Breakfasts professional and critical;

Lunches and snacks so aldermanic
    That one would furnish forth ten dinners,
Where reigns a Cretan-tonguèd panic,
Lest news Russ, Dutch or Alemannic
    Should make some losers, and some winners; –

At conversazioni – balls –
    Conventicles – and drawing-rooms –
Courts of law – committees – calls
Of a morning – clubs – bookstalls –
    Churches – masquerades – and tombs.

And this is Hell – and in this smother
    All are damnable and damned;
Each one damning, damns the other;
They are damned by one another,
    By none other are they damned.

Song to the Men of England

Men of England, wherefore plough
For the lords who lay ye low?
Wherefore weave with toil and care
The rich robes your tyrants wear?

Wherefore feed, and clothe, and save,
From the cradle to the grave,
Those ungrateful drones who would
Drain your sweat – nay, drink your blood?

Wherefore, Bees of England, forge
Many a weapon, chain, and scourge,
That these stingless drones may spoil
The forced produce of your toil?

Have ye leisure, comfort, calm,
Shelter, food, love's gentle balm?
Or what is it ye buy so dear
With your pain and with your fear?

The seed ye sow, another reaps;
The wealth ye find, another keeps;
The robes ye weave, another wears;
The arms ye forge, another bears.

Sow seed, – but let no tyrant reap;
Find wealth, – let no impostor heap;
Weave robes, – let not the idle wear;
Forge arms, – in your defence bear.

Shrink to your cellars, holes, and cells;
In halls ye deck another dwells.
Why shake the chains ye wrought? Ye see
The steel ye tempered glance on ye.

With plough and spade, and hoe and loom,
Trace your grave, and build your tomb,
And weave your winding-sheet, till fair
England be your sepulchre.

Lines to a Critic

Honey from silkworms who can gather,
Or silk from the yellow bee?
The grass may grow in winter weather
As soon as hate in me.

Hate men who cant, and men who pray,
And men who rail like thee;
An equal passion to repay
They are not coy like me.

Or seek some slave of power and gold
To be thy dear heart's mate;
Thy love will move that bigot cold
Sooner than me, thy hate.

A passion like the one I prove
Cannot divided be;
I hate thy want of truth and love –
How should I then hate thee?

Sonnet: England in 1819

An old, mad, blind, despised, and dying king, –
Princes, the dregs of their dull race, who flow
Through public scorn, – mud from a muddy
    spring, –
Rulers who neither see, nor feel, nor know,
But leech-like to their fainting country cling,
Till they drop, blind in blood, without a blow, –
A people starved and stabbed in the untilled
    field, –
An army, which liberticide and prey
Makes as a two-edged sword to all who wield, –
Golden and sanguine laws which tempt and slay;
Religion Christless, Godless – a book sealed;
A Senate, – Time's worst statute unrepealed, –
Are graves, from which a glorious Phantom may
Burst, to illumine our tempestuous day.

From
LINES WRITTEN AMONG THE EUGANEAN HILLS

Beneath is spread like a green sea
The waveless plain of Lombardy,
Bounded by the vaporous air,
Islanded by cities fair;
Underneath Day's azure eyes
Ocean's nursling, Venice lies,
A peopled labyrinth of walls,
Amphitrite's destined halls,
Which her hoary sire now paves
With his blue and beaming waves.
Lo! the sun upsprings behind,
Broad, red, radiant, half-reclined
On the level quivering line
Of the waters crystalline;
And before that chasm of light,
As within a furnace bright,
Column, tower, and dome, and spire,
Shine like obelisks of fire,
Pointing with inconstant motion
From the altar of dark ocean
To the sapphire-tinted skies;
As the flames of sacrifice
From the marble shrines did rise,
As to pierce the dome of gold
Where Apollo spoke of old.

Sun-girt City, thou hast been
Ocean's child, and then his queen;
Now is come a darker day,
And thou soon must be his prey,
If the power that raised thee here
Hallow so thy watery bier.
A less drear ruin then than now,
With thy conquest-branded brow
Stooping to the slave of slaves
From thy throne, among the waves
Wilt thou be, when the sea-mew
Flies, as once before it flew,
O'er thine isles depopulate,
And all is in its ancient state,
Save where many a palace gate
With green sea-flowers overgrown
Like a rock of Ocean's own
Topples o'er the abandoned sea
As the tides change sullenly.
The fisher on his watery way,
Wandering at the close of day,
Will spread his sail and seize his oar
Till he pass the gloomy shore,
Lest thy dead should, from their sleep
Bursting o'er the starlight deep,
Lead a rapid masque of death
O'er the waters of his path.

Stanzas Written in Dejection, Near Naples

The sun is warm, the sky is clear,
    The waves are dancing fast and bright,
Blue isles and snowy mountains wear
    The purple noon's transparent might,
    The breath of the moist earth is light,
Around its unexpanded buds;
    Like many a voice of one delight,
The winds, the birds, the ocean floods,
The City's voice itself, is soft like Solitude's.

I see the Deep's untrampled floor
    With green and purple seaweeds strown;
I see the waves upon the shore,
    Like light dissolved in star-showers, thrown:
    I sit upon the sands alone, –
The lightning of the noontide ocean
    Is flashing round me, and a tone
Arises from its measured motion,
How sweet! did any heart now share in my
    emotion.

Alas! I have nor hope nor health,
    Nor peace within nor calm around,
Nor that content surpassing wealth
    The sage in meditation found,
    And walked with inward glory crowned –

Nor fame, nor power, nor love, nor leisure.
　　Others I see whom these surround –
Smiling they live, and call life pleasure; –
To me that cup has been dealt in another
　　measure.

Yet now despair itself is mild,
　　Even as the winds and water are;
I could lie down like a tired child,
　　And weep away this life of care
　　Which I have borne and yet must bear,
Till death like sleep might steal on me,
　　And I might feel in the warm air
My cheek grow cold, and hear the sea
Breathe o'er my dying brain its last monotony.

Some might lament that I were cold,
　　As I, when this sweet day is gone,
Which my lost heart, too soon grown cold,
　　Insults with this untimely moan;
　　They might lament – for I am one
Whom men love not, – and yet regret,
　　Unlike this day, which, when the sun
Shall on its stainless glory set,
Will linger, though enjoyed, like joy in memory
　　yet.

From JULIAN AND MADDALO

Thou Paradise of exiles, Italy!
Thy mountains, seas, and vineyards, and the
    towers
Of cities they encircle! – it was ours
To stand on thee, beholding it: and then,
Just where we had dismounted, the Count's men
Were waiting for us with the gondola, –
As those who pause on some delightful way
Though bent on pleasant pilgrimage, we stood
Looking upon the evening, and the flood
Which lay between the city and the shore,
Paved with the image of the sky ... the hoar
And aëry Alps towards the North appeared
Through mist, an heaven-sustaining bulwark
    reared
Between the East and West; and half the sky
Was roofed with clouds of rich emblazonry
Dark purple at the zenith, which still grew
Down the steep West into a wondrous hue
Brighter than burning gold, even to the rent
Where the swift sun yet paused in his descent
Among the many-folded hills: they were
Those famous Euganean hills, which bear,
As seen from Lido thro' the harbour piles,
The likeness of a clump of peakèd isles –

And then – as if the Earth and Sea had been
Dissolved into one lake of fire, were seen
Those mountains towering as from waves of flame
Around the vaporous sun, from which there came
The inmost purple spirit of light, and made
Their very peaks transparent. 'Ere it fade,'
Said my companion, 'I will show you soon
A better station' – so, o'er the lagune
We glided; and from that funereal bark
I leaned, and saw the city, and could mark
How from their many isles, in evening's gleam,
Its temples and its palaces did seem
Like fabrics of enchantment piled to Heaven.

With a Guitar, to Jane

Ariel to Miranda: – Take
This slave of Music, for the sake
Of him who is the slave of thee,
And teach it all the harmony
In which thou canst, and only thou,
Make the delighted spirit glow,
Till joy denies itself again,
And, too intense, is turned to pain;
For by permission and command
Of thine own Prince Ferdinand,
Poor Ariel sends this silent token
Of more than ever can be spoken;
Your guardian spirit, Ariel, who,
From life to life, must still pursue
Your happiness; – for thus alone
Can Ariel ever find his own.
From Prospero's enchanted cell,
As the mighty verses tell,
To the throne of Naples, he
Lit you o'er the trackless sea,
Flitting on, your prow before,
Like a living meteor.
When you die, the silent Moon,
In her interlunar swoon,
Is not sadder in her cell
Than deserted Ariel.
When you live again on earth,
Like an unseen star of birth,

Ariel guides you o'er the sea
Of life from your nativity.
Many changes have been run
Since Ferdinand and you begun
Your course of love, and Ariel still
Has tracked your steps, and served your will;
Now, in humbler, happier lot,
This is all remembered not;
And now, alas! the poor sprite is
Imprisoned, for some fault of his,
In a body like a grave; –
From you he only dares to crave,
For his service and his sorrow,
A smile to-day, a song to-morrow.
The artist who this idol wrought,
To echo all harmonious thought,
Felled a tree, while on the steep
The woods were in their winter sleep,
Rocked in that repose divine
On the wind-swept Apennine;
And dreaming, some of Autumn past,
And some of Spring approaching fast,
And all of love; and so this tree, –
O that such our death may be! –
Died in sleep, and felt no pain,
To live in happier form again:
From which, beneath Heaven's fairest star,
The artist wrought this loved Guitar,
And taught it justly to reply,
To all who question skilfully,

In language gentle as thine own;
Whispering in enamoured tone
Sweet oracles of woods and dells,
And summer winds in sylvan cells;
For it had learned all harmonies
Of the plains and of the skies,
Of the forests and the mountains,
And the many-voicèd fountains;
The clearest echoes of the hills,
The softest notes of falling rills,
The melodies of birds and bees,
The murmuring of summer seas,
And pattering rain, and breathing dew,
And airs of evening; and it knew
That seldom-heard mysterious sound,
Which, driven on its diurnal round,
As it floats through boundless day,
Our world enkindles on its way. –
All this it knows, but will not tell
To those who cannot question well
The Spirit that inhabits it;
It talks according to the wit
Of its companions; and no more
Is heard than has been felt before,
By those who tempt it to betray
These secrets of an elder day:
But, sweetly as its answers will
Flatter hands of perfect skill,
It keeps its highest, holiest tone
For our belovèd Jane alone.

From
THE BOAT ON THE SERCHIO

Our boat is asleep on Serchio's stream,
Its sails are folded like thoughts in a dream,
The helm sways idly, hither and thither;
    Dominic, the boatman, has brought the mast,
    And the oars, and the sails; but 'tis sleeping
        fast,
Like a beast, unconscious of its tether.

The stars burnt out in the pale blue air,
And the thin white moon lay withering there:
To tower, and cavern, and rift, and tree,
The owl and the bat fled drowsily.
Day had kindled the dewy woods,
    And the rocks above and the stream below,
And the vapours in their multitudes,
    And the Apennine's shroud of summer snow,
And clothed with light of aëry gold
The mists in their eastern caves uprolled.

Day had awakened all things that be,
The lark and the thrush and the swallow free,
    And the milkmaid's song and the mower's
        scythe,
And the matin-bell and the mountain bee:
Fireflies were quenched on the dewy corn,

Glow-worms went out on the river's brim,
   Like lamps which a student forgets to trim:
The beetle forgot to wind his horn,
   The crickets were still in the meadow and hill:
Like a flock of rooks at a farmer's gun
Night's dreams and terrors, every one,
Fled from the brains which are their prey
From the lamp's death to the morning ray.

All rose to do the task He set to each,
   Who shaped us to His ends and not our own;
The million rose to learn, and one to teach
   What none yet ever knew or can be known.
     And many rose
   Whose woe was such that fear became desire; –
Melchior and Lionel were not among those;
They from the throng of men had stepped aside,
And made their home under the green hill-side.
It was that hill, whose intervening brow
   Screens Lucca from the Pisan's envious eye,
Which the circumfluous plain waving below,
   Like a wide lake of green fertility,
With streams and fields and marshes bare,
   Divides from the far Apennines – which lie
Islanded in the immeasurable air.

From ADONAIS

An Elegy on the
Death of John Keats

He has outsoared the shadow of our night;
Envy and calumny and hate and pain,
And that unrest which men miscall delight,
Can touch him not and torture not again;
From the contagion of the world's slow stain
He is secure, and now can never mourn
A heart grown cold, a head grown gray in vain;
Nor, when the spirit's self has ceased to burn
With sparkless ashes load an unlamented urn.

He lives, he wakes – 'tis Death is dead, not he;
Mourn not for Adonais. – Thou young Dawn,
Turn all thy dew to splendour, for from thee
The spirit thou lamentest is not gone;
Ye caverns and ye forests, cease to moan!
Cease, ye faint flowers and fountains, and thou
    Air,
Which like a mourning veil thy scarf hadst
    thrown
O'er the abandoned Earth, now leave it bare
Even to the joyous stars which smile on its
    despair!

He is made one with Nature: there is heard
His voice in all her music, from the moan
Of thunder, to the song of night's sweet bird;
He is a presence to be felt and known
In darkness and in light, from herb and stone,
Spreading itself where'er that Power may move
Which has withdrawn his being to its own;
Which wields the world with never-wearied
      love,
Sustains it from beneath, and kindles it above.

The One remains, the many change and pass;
Heaven's light forever shines, Earth's shadows
    fly;
Life, like a dome of many-coloured glass
Stains the white radiance of Eternity,
Until Death tramples it to fragments. – Die,
If thou wouldst be with that which thou dost
    seek!
Follow where all is fled! – Rome's azure sky,
Flowers, ruins, statues, music, words, are weak
The glory they transfuse with fitting truth to
    speak.

The breath whose might I have invoked in song
Descends on me; my spirit's bark is driven,
Far from the shore, far from the trembling
    throng
Whose sails were never to the tempest given;
The massy earth and spherèd skies are riven!
I am borne darkly, fearfully, afar;
Whilst, burning through the inmost veil of
    Heaven,
The soul of Adonais, like a star,
Beacons from the abode where the Eternal are.

From THE TRIUMPH OF LIFE

The Grove

Grew dense with shadows to its inmost covers,
The earth was gray with phantoms, and the air
Was peopled with dim forms, as when there
    hovers

A flock of vampire-bats before the glare
Of the tropic sun, bringing, ere evening,
Strange night upon some Indian isle; – thus were

Phantoms diffused around; and some did fling
Shadows of shadows, yet unlike themselves,
Behind them; some like eaglets on the wing

Were lost in the white day; others like elves
Danced in a thousand unimagined shapes
Upon the sunny streams and grassy shelves;

And others sate chattering like restless apes
On vulgar hands, …
Some made a cradle of the ermined capes

Of kingly mantles; some across the tiar
Of pontiffs sate like vultures; others played
Under the crown which girt with empire

A baby's or an idiot's brow, and made
Their nests in it. The old anatomies
Sate hatching their bare broods under the shade

Of daemon wings, and laughed from their dead
        eyes
To reassume the delegated power,
Arrayed in which those worms did monarchize,

Who made this earth their charnel. Others more
Humble, like falcons, sate upon the fist
Of common men, and round their heads did soar;

Or like small gnats and flies, as thick as mist
On evening marshes, thronged about the brow
Of lawyers, statesmen, priest and theorist; –

And others, like discoloured flakes of snow
On fairest bosoms and the sunniest hair,
Fell, and were melted by the youthful glow

Which they extinguished; and, like tears, they
        were
A veil to those from whose faint lids they rained
In drops of sorrow.

SOURCES OF THE EXTRACTS

Prometheus Unbound, Fourth Spirit's Song, Act 1, lines 737 to 749.
Epipsychidion, lines 130 to 173.
The Revolt of Islam, Canto 8, stanzas 14, 15, 16.
The Cenci, Act 5, Scene 4, lines 97 to 118.
The Mask of Anarchy, stanzas 1 to 12.
Peter Bell the Third, Part Three, stanzas 1, 2, 4, 5, 6, 7, 9, 10, 12.
'Lines Written Among the Euganean Hills', lines 90 to 141.
'Julian and Maddalo', lines 57 to 92.
'With a Guitar, to Jane': the following lines, being parenthetical, have
　　been excised from the text (at line 50) for reasons of space:
　　'And some of April buds and showers,
　　And some of songs in July bowers,'
'The Boat on the Serchio', lines 1 to 45.
Adonais, stanzas 40, 41, 42, 52, 55.
The Triumph of Life, lines 480 to 515.

NOTES ON THE PICTURES

p. 6   *Mary Wollstonecraft Shelley* by Richard Rothwell (1800–68). National Portrait Gallery, London.

p. 15   *Study of Sea and Sky* by John Constable (1776–1837). Christie's, London. Photo: Bridgeman Art Library, London.

p. 19   *The Birth of Venus* (detail) by Sandro Botticelli (1444–1510). Uffizi Gallery, Florence.

p. 23   *Liberty Leading the People* by Eugène Delacroix (1798–1863). Louvre, Paris.

p. 26   *The Sphinx* (detail) by Sir David Young Cameron (1865–1945). Fine Art Society, London.

p. 31   *Charing Cross: The Pillory* by Thomas Rowlandson (1756/7–1827). Reproduced by courtesy of the Board of Trustees of the Victoria and Albert Museum, London.

p. 35   *The Haymakers* by George Stubbs (1724–1806). National Museums and Galleries on Merseyside; Lady Lever Art Gallery, Port Sunlight.

p. 38   Caricature of George IV, 'A *Voluptuary Under the Horrors of Digestion*' by James Gillray (1757–1815). National Portrait Gallery, London.

p. 43   *Bay of Naples* by Franz Richard Unterberger (1838–1902). Photo: Fine Art Photographic Library, London.

p. 46   *Venice, The Salute* by Thomas Bush Hardy (1842–97). Photo: Fine Art Photographic Library, London.

p. 50   *The Bay of Baiae, with Apollo and the Sibyl* (detail) by J.M.W. Turner (1775–1851). Tate Gallery, London.

p. 54   *Peace: Burial at Sea* by J.M.W. Turner (1775–1851). Tate Gallery, London.

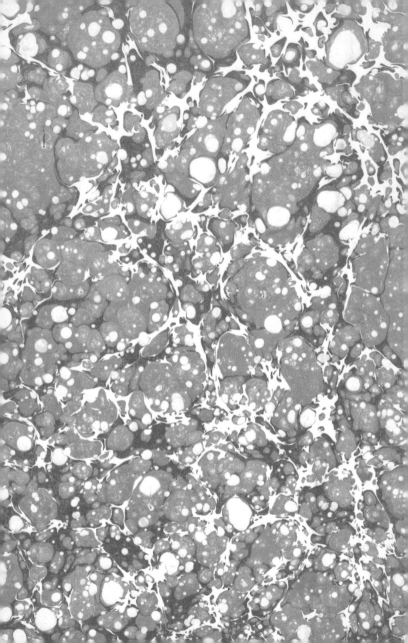